Lino Milita

Mutual Rebirths

Youcanprint *Self-Publishing*

Title | Mutual Rebirths
Author | Lino Milita
Cover by Diego Luci
ISBN | 978-88-91197-48-1

Copyright © 2015 Lino Milita - All rights reserved

Original title: *Reciproche Rinascite*. Translated from the Italian by Diego Luci, www.diegoluci.it.

Cover image by Samanta Lai: *Tai Chi*.
For the other images read the section *Photo Credits*.

No part of this book may be reproduced without the consent of the Author.

Special thanks to Stella Demaris for the layout of the book.
stella-demaris.blogspot.it

Youcanprint Self-Publishing
Via Roma, 73-73039 Tricase (LE) - Italy
+39 / 0832.1836509
Fax +39 / 0832.1836533
www.youcanprint.it
info@youcanprint.it
Facebook: facebook.com / youcanprint.it
Twitter: twitter.com / youcanprintit

Lino Milita

After my first book of poetry and images *Sogni Sospesi* (*Hanging Dreams*), here I am again with another appointment with myself, to propose you a new share of moods and events of everyday life.

The offer is discreet, because a rebirth denying the past and, with it, all the experiences affecting your life until now, cannot be considered a true rebirth. My assumption is that a revival is always collective, thus it may represent a genuine and radical transformation.

www.linomilita.com/en

lino.milita@gmail.com

Translator's Note

Translating poetry is a challenging work when you have to render a metric rule in a different one, or to respect the original scheme of rhymes with dissonant alien nouns.

Lino Milita's poetry does not follow any metrical rule: thoughts and feelings induced by words are the only concern of the author, to suggest and recreate moods through discord and imbalance.

Nevertheless, his fondness for oxymoron, the use of discordant adjectives and the drift to hermetism that mark his poetry had to be restored in English carefully, avoiding to decrypt it either too much or too little, fleeing from a literal translation of Italian affected terms, absolutely odd in an English setting.

I hope you can enjoy this faithful translation and blame me alone for any inaccuracy you could meet.

Diego Luci, June 2015

*To be born again as adults,
without pain...*

Contents

Invitations 13

For You 15

Balances 17

The Offer We Are 19

Evoked Shadows 21

The Promise of Awakening 23

Awakening 25

Openings 27

Suffered Invites 29

You and I 31

Cupid and Psyche 33

Serene Night 35

Peaceful Renouncements 37

Take Me Back With You 39

Builder of Worlds 41

Sunny Awakening 43

You 45

Happy Excitement 47

Male 49

Cheeks 51

Hesitations 53

The Touch of the World 55

Lies of Nothing 57

In Arid Delay 59

Static Silences 61

Lost Promises 63

Woman in Autumn 65

Epitaph for My Shadow 67

Each Other Alone 69

Desire 71

In the Core of Unreflective Black 73

Fallen Hopes 75

Rebirths 77

The Beginning and the End 79

Rebirths 81

Embryonic Orbits 83

Woman 85

Free Births 87

My Smile 89

The Infinite Source 91

To the Generated Fathers 93

I'd Dare to Be a Father 95

The Announcement 97

Networks of Reality 99

Common Compassion 101

Veils of the Night 103

Winds of Blue Relief 105

Don't Give Up 107

Naked Faces 109

Assonances 111

Cosmogony 113

Let the Tear Happen 115

Praise to the Free Day 117

Biographical Notes about the Artists 119

Photo Credits 125

OTHER WORKS BY LINO MILITA, PUBLISHED IN ITALIAN 129

Invitations

For You

With cloths of indolent air
I move the lull with you,
to browse wires
of tired cradles.

We open butterfly wings
between demure evolutions,
to support the star
with anaemic pulse.

We regenerate bitter hours
with the oblique scattered orbits
to arouse blind colourless airs
from a dried up waiting.

Hilma af Klint, *Svanen*

Balances

True dreams, placed in real vigils,
are pushed on by wandering voices in thin foils
of the solar path, that takes away to them
blacks veils of forgetfulness.

Rough commitments induce profitable aims,
offering visions of a calculating eye
while requiring imperious and productive uses
of greedy confidence.

Ritual courtesies of forced exchanges
mime the oblique dance of the diurnal rays,
replicating postures in combined bonds
of arid quibbles.

Mutable labels require embryos of events
from nocturnal hefty words,
consolidating generous senses and eloquent
elementary actions.

Minute evaluations, wedged at the borders
of logic war conflicts, oscillate
in an erotic dance of golden, darkened
debris.

For all this we evoke effusions from the volcano
of dreamlike fermentation, while offering

cadences and scheduled rules that sneak off
from unreal yokes.

Therefore we reconcile lazy stops
between moist white air and cool rural green,
thence absorbed and leisured we assure them
a fair nourishment.

Susana Ragel Nieto, *Tumbada*

The Offer We Are

We are convinced to act as scattered grains
through meaningless dances,
suffering fears from an uncertain absence
in the illusion of nothing

and

we do not observe the borderless ocean
that overflows from childish ego's networks,
offering infinite destinies amidst
recent opening pages.

Yarek Godfrey, *Dawn and Dusk*

Evoked Shadows

Winged celestial bows radiate calls
to underground eyes,
obscuring memories of swarms
of ancient candour now emptied.

Renegade invitations implore
the deaf and reclined heart,
so as to receive shadows emerging
from a mutual caused pain.

Listen, then, to a fair plea
of desire despised
by an archaic rancour: it indicates
to everybody his golden destiny.

Caspar David Friedrich,
Woman Before the Setting Sun

The Promise of Awakening

Sleeping angel
of neglected expectations,

you are still waiting
for your wished gift.

Finally your wings
are no longer avoided by your heart.

From an igneous shape and
from your hair now opening freely,

you appear as
a future promise.

Johann Heinrich Füssli, *The Silence*

Awakening

Surprised for the life's gift to my soul,
brilliant first and in conveniently autonomy after,
the lost iris at the new light I reopen
by shiny liquid in the veil I discover.

During the yellow morning quietly in laugh,
I get used to the frail care of colours
to avoid the indifferent erased kiss,
holding fast in the humid halo that keeps fears away.

Wake me up, my love... and enlighten my face
enshrouded by the night in secure coils
of childhood hesitation, to dream of myself unbroken.

By the amniotic pearls that you had as a gift,
welcome my sweaty hands resurfaced,
stretched towards yours so firm and strong.

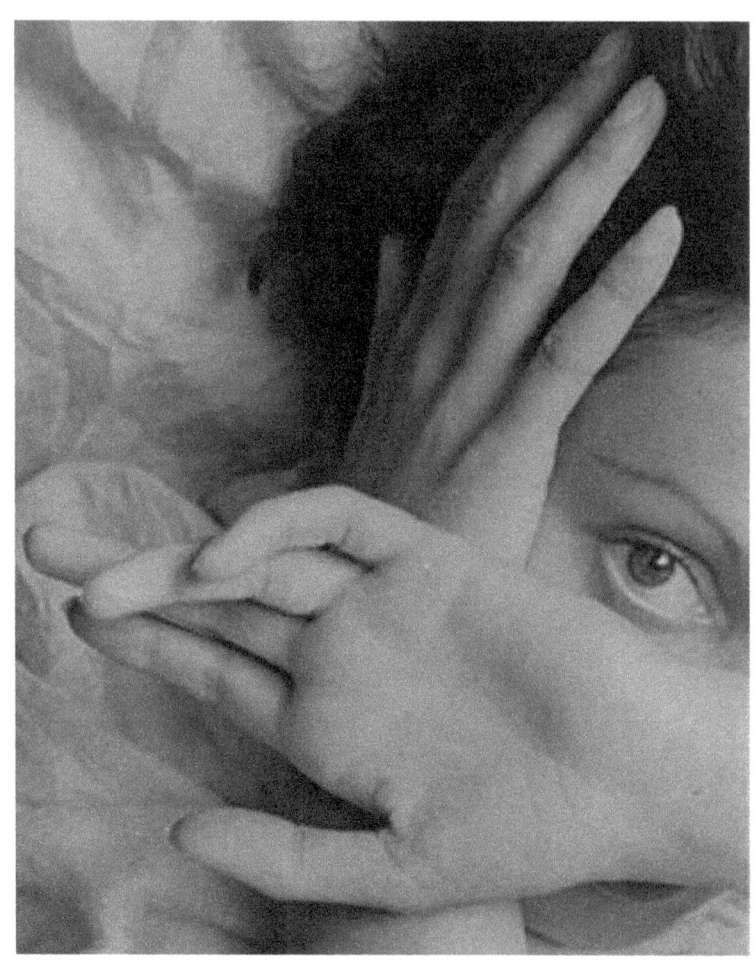

Erwin Blumenfeld, *Eyes of Youth*

Openings

When she opens her eyes to the rocking cradle of the world,
she raises the glassy bow of the horizon,
to set up the reciting proscenium,
as an invitation to the dream of the stirred hope.

When I'll be in front of the image filmed
by the bodily appearance guarded,
the splintered vision will be reunited
in a perspective of common alliance.

The indistinct cloud of evoked memories
that I am, in custody at the oblivion gates,
is thickened at the contact with your ciliated kisses.

For each call of loving and generous opening
temporal substrates trace points
to embody the promise still locked up.

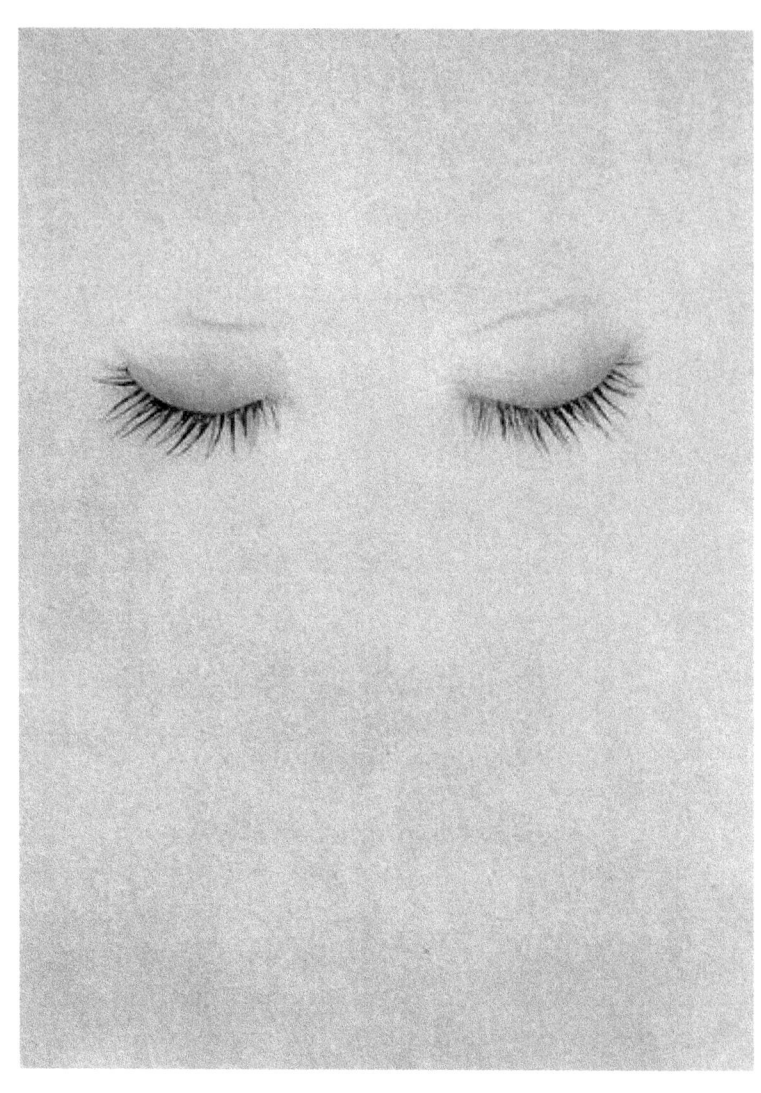

Erwin Blumenfeld, *Eyes Closed*

Suffered Invites

In the tearful cuts
of bloody arrows
with painful lightning,

for each one a demand
you observe, through the eye that spits
and the annoying mouth.

What horror shall I feel,
so as I can speak?

Man Ray, *Air Mata*

You and I

In this uncertain encounter, for necrotic
father's prayers, made of hypocrite prohibitions
and angry obligations with cyanotic chatter,
we met.

Weak whims, by words plundered
and concealed, for sensations buried
by pompous and erect rules, were questioned
without any care.

Neglected nightmares, of anxious wedged
warnings, advocates of childish
and foolish urges: they emanated
ignoble pains, while being so enmeshed.

Avoided fears, for rough notes
of amber tokens, for inverted emotions
now contrasted: we said goodbye to them,
with mutual eyes.

Lonely steps, no longer observed
by greedy shepherds offering
rituals lambs, with consonant rhythms
we exchanged each other.

Naked voices, by suspended questions
created by our naive eyes evoke,
with soft touches and red cheeks,
that you and I are in love.

Man Ray, *The Kiss*

Cupid and Psyche

The thin look
of a willing mind
for mutual ecstasy
with a sharp dart,

opens the free hearts
in golden wishes
divided by a cut,

in the feared time
of the Olympian envious god...

But now the erotic erosion,
of hateful division,
rewinds the inversion.

Antonio Canova, *Cupid and Psyche*

Serene Night

I watch over you,
but not as a malevolent
father who, for each
painful look,
evokes a command
of unlucky possession.

I watch into your eye
made of desired
veiled dreams
of ancient shyness,
for promises
given and now delivered.

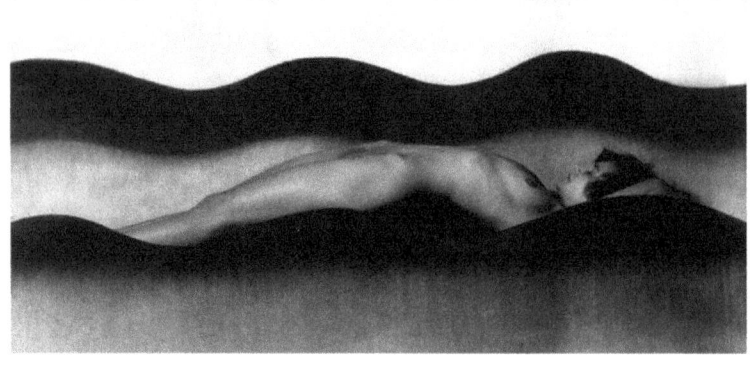

František Drtikoln, *Wave*

Peaceful Renouncements

In yokes made of igneous curves,

granted memories
cleave acid drops
of purple waves,

for grim jealousies,

in thirsty horizons
that change pale
rocks in dry rivers.

Enclosed tones
of harmonious pains
delete messages
of rejected offers
for separate bows;

however, on the thresholds,
I hope to renounce
to walled-up ties.

Jean-Frédéric Bazille, *Portrait de Pierre-Auguste Renoir*

Take Me Back With You

Don't harden your heart
for the brutal thrill
due to passing lies
on a desolate body,
while waiting, such as marble,
an unexpected return.

Raise the unvoiced alcove
from the intentional wounds,
a tangle of nervous brambles
unfolded in an isolated union.
Rise up from that flowerbed
so naive and frozen.

By rabid hate
of my vile desertion,
accept, by the wet iris,
godlike omens of
required forgiveness:
take me back with you as a man.

Giacomo Balla, *The Girlfriend at the Pincio*

Builder of Worlds

What tidings do you offer us,
builder of worlds?

Beyond the event horizon
you're drawing and arranging
this further eternity.

Wish and welcome us
in the fluid new dawn
of our lives and in those of others'.

Jacob Christian Poen de Wijs, *House in France*

Sunny Awakening

Awake, watching polychrome hours
in the care of a filial sleep,
in a vigilant bow of optical beam
towards events of your adventures,
I revere my heart like a homage.

Let it be, father! But in the wake
you'll become a tree with a little shade,
in a damp nest of small wings.
Oh, brother, out of the bed
you are and fly free in the air.

Jean Hippolyte Flandrin, *Polytès, fils de Priam, observant les mouvements des Grecs vers Troie*

You

You reappeared without notices
enshrined with right appeals.

Iridescent sounds of an image
joined to an apathetic wall
removed the dark veil,
gifting a new origin.

Quiet, planted suggestions
placed me
inside a friendly sheath,
diverting my dizziness.

Writing harmonic rhymes in verses
I may sail
to the active afternoon,
to reveal gloomy souls.

Exposing new offers
of consoling abandonment,
I open assonant hugs
for resuscitated hopes.

François-Auguste-René Rodin, *The Eternal Idol*

Happy Excitement

I want, I want an amazing and understandable desire
to be yours, completely yours, totally yours
with no petition, no omission, no remission
to write now, that's coming from inside, just now.
With no control, no subterfuge, no overpower.

I want, I want an inexhaustible and inextinguishable desire
to be yours, of course yours, naturally yours
with all myself shown, dedicated and by you invited.

A desire, a desire drunk and clear to be born
as your son and then your adult and your lover.
I want, I want now a hug without worry
to grow in copulation, in common permission,
without petition, no claim, no oppression.

Simeon Solomon, *For the Night Must Pass Before the Coming Day*

Male

Male,
in soundless search
of a believed lack.

Blind,
in the dazzle of adjectives
I'm calling you with earthly objects.

Incomplete,
in the miserable aim
of obscene possession.

Devoid
of amniotic ties,
I attract you by timorous ethics.

Sad,
for insufficient coin
in the emptied trunk.

Prone,
for primitive fears,
I wait for you with no blunt weapons.

Woman,
your role demolished
by my rude speaking,
I ask you
the onerous gesture that can show
how much I am made of you.

Yves Klein, *Invisible*

Cheeks

Cheeks
as
expected
companions,
seen as
wineskins
folded:
they remember
always,
in
speechless
melancholy,
to be
the second
ear
for a sweet
gift
of a modest
echo.

Pruett Carter, *Unknown Title*

Hesitations

The Touch of the World

Calls of repeated omnipresence
and visions of stretched absence
defer sensorial meetings, desired
by someone different from me in irresolute times.

Techniques of symmetric architecture
struggle in a distracted and sour suture,
to frame unaware and unstable hinges,
incapable to connect to flawless orders.

Echoless researches dissolve a silly selfish desire
towards a deceptive and impossible becoming,
different from the image of a social climber ego:

but foggy clouds of aerated tears
invite the disenchanted to offer a pledge
with an open and mutual unarmed limb.

Silvana Giordano, *Hands*

Lies of Nothing

Reinvented lies
I had again,
weak and masked;

illustrated illusions
I've heard,
useless and disguised;

but you, hypnotic nothing,
of the fairy tales are
the most foolish.

Jean-Joseph Perraud, *Le Désespoir*

In Arid Delay

By hard cracks of air
I arrive into your angry
voluntary thirst.

Lingering with sad hiccups,
in humble listening I admire you
in your last tumults.

Raoul Ubac, *Portrait dans un miroir*

Static Silences

Here I am in my isolated soul,
listening with sealed eyes
obscene and saddened,

helpless and hurt
in the viscous instant
of illicit coitus:

but still I am waiting for
a sudden kiss
in an intense hug.

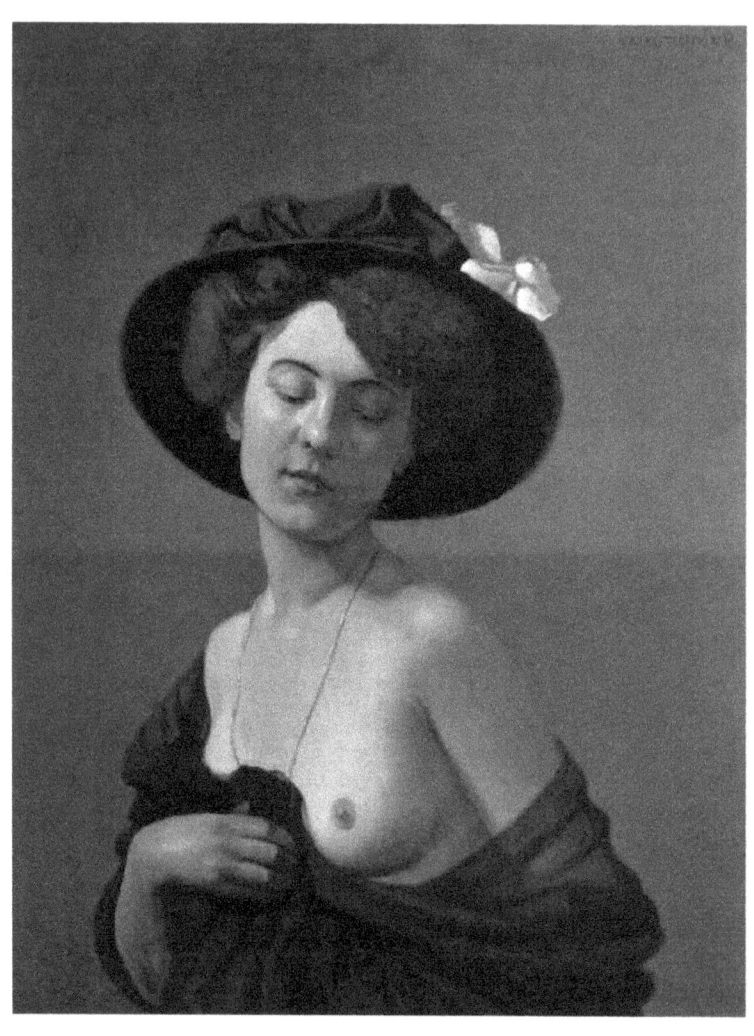

Félix Vallotton, *The Woman with the Black Hat*

Lost Promises

Memories of dusty embroideries,
transcribed in plots, I don't see anymore,
in dry and weary streams
greedy for your kisses in which I still believe.

Turbulent tremors, for tensions
coming from bold encounters, were fed
with exclusive and secret confessions
fastened by sincere intentions.

The silent loops of the rejected
drops of desire for you,
now appear deaf and dried.

In the rough missing answers
lie the sad and weary offers,
hoping to be refreshed.

Friedrich von Amerling, *The Young Girl*

Woman in Autumn

Briarwoods sprayed
by winter violets
you offer to sleepy
spiky arteries.

Weighted cirrus
you reject in expanses
full of beats
of silly agreements.

Sudden gifts
of damp denials,
to my eyes, you cause
in neglected expedients.

Dante Gabriel Rossetti, *Proserpine*

Epitaph for My Shadow

Burned branches flow into hoary supports,
for anaemic memories due to expired notices,
made by migrant wings, lost from piers,
without return from diverted routes.

And before falling into an ice sleep,
into crude obtuse reflection, stingy of awakening,
I hesitate, without a shadow of air, disgusted and forgetful
with a prudent fear in a trembling panic.

From the advent of the footprint of unlucky value,
by perfidious promises to an exhausted pride,
I reject the mouldy limbs along with wrathful pains,
to erase the gaunt useless relics.

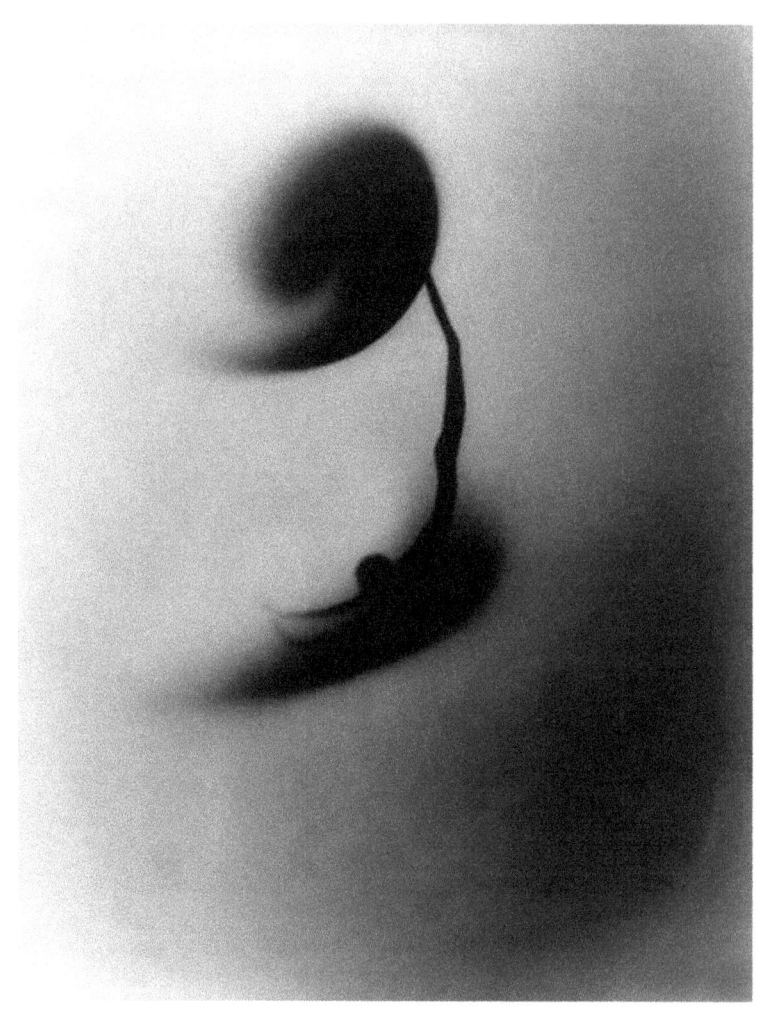

František Drtikol, *Painting*

Each Other Alone

Downcast eyes in soul's nights
leave arid flotsam on the shore,
in a loving, alive union,
smashed by an anonymous hug.

The small and sterile fellowship,
from unnecessary and elusive tides
revolving like aerial waves,
is troubled by a toneless agony.

Deceptive chains separate
airs ecstatically awaited,
of innocent denied strokes
by unkind rough gesture,

but the silent lament of the hot
heart, gloomy like an ungrateful
scream of blurred pain,
feels every shy fear of yours.

Gwen John, *Portrait of Chloe Boughton Leigh*

Desire

The liaison requires
unfailing impositions
in union rituals
of certified
fellowship.

Here are
emotional times
of turning mood
and
thin distances,
in a scattered action,
drain desires
of devoted union.

Complicated void
by harsh crack
for a future fear
and
the outcast anguish
of doubtful chills,
in fact,

invoke weak
sweetness tempting
the drowned arms

to resume a mutual
moment for the emerged,
happy relationship.

Franz von Stuck, *The Sphinx'Kiss*

In the Core of Unreflective Black

Self-propelled wires,
dried by hemispherical cycles
of scattered rays
in cold afternoons,
advance in the undulating
body in the precipice thirsty
of inert arms
and of thoughts under threat...

Yet the dark backdrop,
inebriated by the hard event
of a moody fall,
for the insecure advent
of the crucial passion,
nothing can do for the unquenchable
spark of last suffering
which restarts the solar path.

Alexander Mijáilovich Rodchenko, *Glass and Light*

Fallen Hopes

Every day I am looking for
a sign evoked
by the eye, coming from
your return.

Hard endures
the silent sign.
Yet I inspect,
brave and sad!

It is a poison
for the alien heart,
the sweet impulse
of useless union.

Alexander Mijáilovich Rodchenko,
Woman with Bare Breasts

Rebirths

The Beginning and the End

Take a rest, my dreams.

My usual company
I will restart at the advent
of weak darkness,

although you are the source
of each elementary regenerated
action.

Janos Laszlo Aldor, *Rêverie*

Rebirths

From the beloved desire you cannot see
the modest and humble hands that soothe
tears dried by distant
refusals, cooled by a soundless echo.

Pride, jealous of arid relics,
livid, mocks the occurred rest,
for demands of a hard search
coming from answers of a recalled wall.

Will the frightened grief regain sense here,
from the cut knot of a lost love,
of a generate, instilled lack of union?

Stripped by the amniotic litany
that surrounds the stubborn and petrified soul:
we are born again from my arms in harmony.

Cesare Laurenti, *Head*

Embryonic Orbits

Reborn by
sweet rotations
and
reflected between
frugal mixtures,

describing
tracings of light
and
declining
undertows of shade,

I emerged more real
in the intimate vision.

Edward Weston, *Nude Floating*

Woman

Here I was born
from a deep post-partum
for the broad desire.

It's the naked echo,
a hidden weeping
from the recalled cut...

And the new ovule
appears vigorous
from the generous neck.

In the return
of inward call,
I grow towards you, my beloved.

Photograph of the French painter Jeanne Hébuterne

Free Births

In the scream's moment we were born,
you and I, in a long embrace
of nine eras, that we had
in liquid and dreamlike stamen.

And your half-closed eyes
with a tear of greeting
open my enclosed smile
in the common welcome.

From our very first gait,
the hug was the unanimous act
towards the world in ourselves protracted.

And in a dawn of identical path,
finally, we are now distinct
and together go through.

Wynn Bullock, *The Mother with Child*

My Smile

Melted by hands soaked of blind
possession and cracked by a sordid echo,
the bells resound, still angry
of calls coming from rough and distant eras.

Roads paved with blood signs
keep a violence that continues
to carve painful ways in my limbs,
obliged to live as waste.

Sculpted dreams and images whitewashed
by the spy of hypocrite laws,
crush the stolen hopes.

And, without owing an explanation to a hostile envious eye,
self-confident in ways of innocent walk,
without marks, I ascend to my smile.

František Drtikol, *Untitled*

The Infinite Source

Curious, I asked for the sudden cause
of the humid curves in an eruptive growth,
with uncertain amazement, of anxious pause,
of an inflamed body in flourishing output.

In the back of the planet's albino shadow,
reflected in the orbits at every igneous, lulled beam,
soothe the imperious secret spring
while feeding the never filled universe.

My apparent degeneration
of giving birth to the liquid origin and
the solid effect, is its evolution.

By double gift, she is everywhere acclaimed
in preserving past and present:
I am the surplus, by future invoked.

Gino Severini, *The Mother*

To the Generated Fathers

Unknown senses were wandering,
around my uneven gait,
for the origin of unspoken fears
and for the uncertain arrival coined by myself.

Ambivalent unconfessed emotions
contradicted feisty postures
from volcanic impulses erupted,
blended by my unusual figures.

Desired mundane questions
cut lazy and usual roots
from the weak images of the past,

but the cry of the anguished infant
by the guardian of my offered juice,
sings that I am reborn too.

Werner Bischof, *Indo-China*

I'd Dare to Be a Father

By a harmonic wave
from the sound of a harp,
I would dare to be taken,
so to overflow every bay
with rejected gifts and
disused memories.

From ropes of water,
in a naked suffering
and in the lost comfort
of hard-working enterprises,
I'm fishing the softly vanished
memories.

Blue abyss
I expect then,
in the midst of
the auroral dawn,
to generate
paternal nights and
promised children.

Fjdelisle, *Coucher de soleil au-dessus du Nil au Caire*

The Announcement

Dedicated to Cetta De Luca

Spread the awakening of unveiled clouds
to accommodate the swift footprint's rays
riding to the thinned out shadows
in a wide expanse.

Fearing to touch the material limbs
impressed in the ancient daytime recall,
we dissolve the need for liar wrappings
of arid claim.

Leave clamours and pressing calls
hesitating between the possible and the vigil,
changing misty lids into embroideries
of golden dew.

Enter with childish limbs in the maternal sea,
caressing the enmeshed veining
of the arid stasis, in order to seek a governance
of careful attention.

Let yourself be absorbed, as a sleeping bond
suspended between two lazy and forgetful lovers,
and in the glare of the eye, slightly,
open yourself to the understanding.

Pay a tribute to the happy song that quenches
and brightens each breath's rhythm,
to be born again remembering every
discrete infatuation.

Armand Point, *Pauline Barrett*
(Edgar Lee Masters)

Networks of Reality

The desires of the possible worlds,
constrained in an alien superficiality,
are weighed as a senescence
that lingers into insoluble lies.

Lazy synthesis judge abstract actions
with childhood fairy tales of magic dawns,
announced by excited butterflies
free to depict aerial desires;

but every consonant, rhythm of wings recalled
in variable openings of awakenings,
opens the mirror of each enlightened petal.

And every encounter of universal wonder,
as a celebration for a new appearance,
takes care of a new and more intense vigil.

Martin Johnson Heade, *Approaching Thunder Storm*

Common Compassion

Like you, I aspire
to him and to her
and to any event that comes

and that restores,
however, in the
hopeless dark,

compassion
as the common
monument
of ancient humanity
that forever we are:

even in the deaf
and deplored oblivion.

Alfred Stiegliz, *Untitled*

Veils of the Night

Veils of the night,
imposed on the universal genre
of the human half,
powerless to obscure
the vivid redness
originating the world
with extreme generosity.

Samanta Lai, *True Life*

Winds of Blue Relief

Winds of blue relief
caress your closed eyes
for intense desire,
with moments of wakefulness,
extending new dreams unsealed
by my eternal creation.

Maxmilián Pirner, *The Sleepwalker*

Don't Give Up

Diaphanous airs,
of unnecessary
words,
shine through
the hibernated
face.

No eye
can rediscover
evoked
desires
by others'
inebriation.

Swollen
masks
and deaf
words
hope
in lunar
dazzles.

The way
of steps
of absent
arrival,

however, I search,
for mutual
courage,

because
quietly
we rest,
threw back
in destinations
promised
by heroic
fancy.

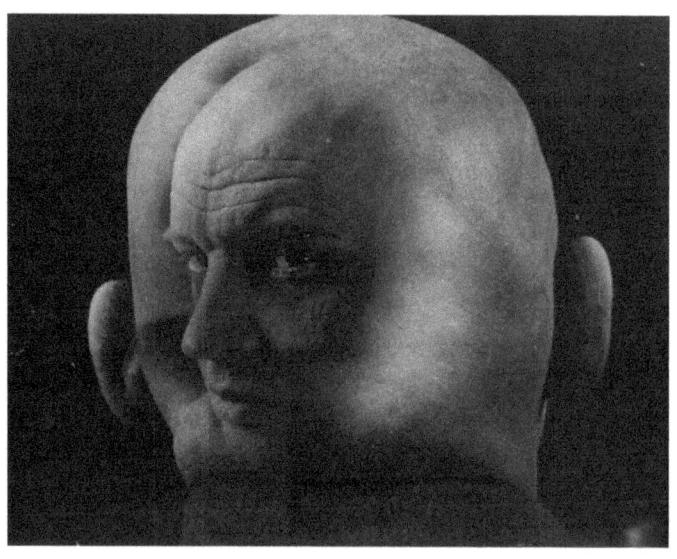

Alexander Mijáilovich Rodchenko,
Medgeorgi Petrusov

Naked Faces

We are made of reasonable purposes
that accompany proud postures,
fed by seductive cultivations
full of improper desires.

Hoping for lazy futile attentions
we surrender to unnecessary lordships,
consumed by wrathful memories
with hands bent to hypocrite absolutions.

Yet we deny childish modesties
of suffering sweetly evoked
by naive moods and irresistible ardours.

And then in the declared union,
without dark and fake tinsels,
the common understanding is knotted again.

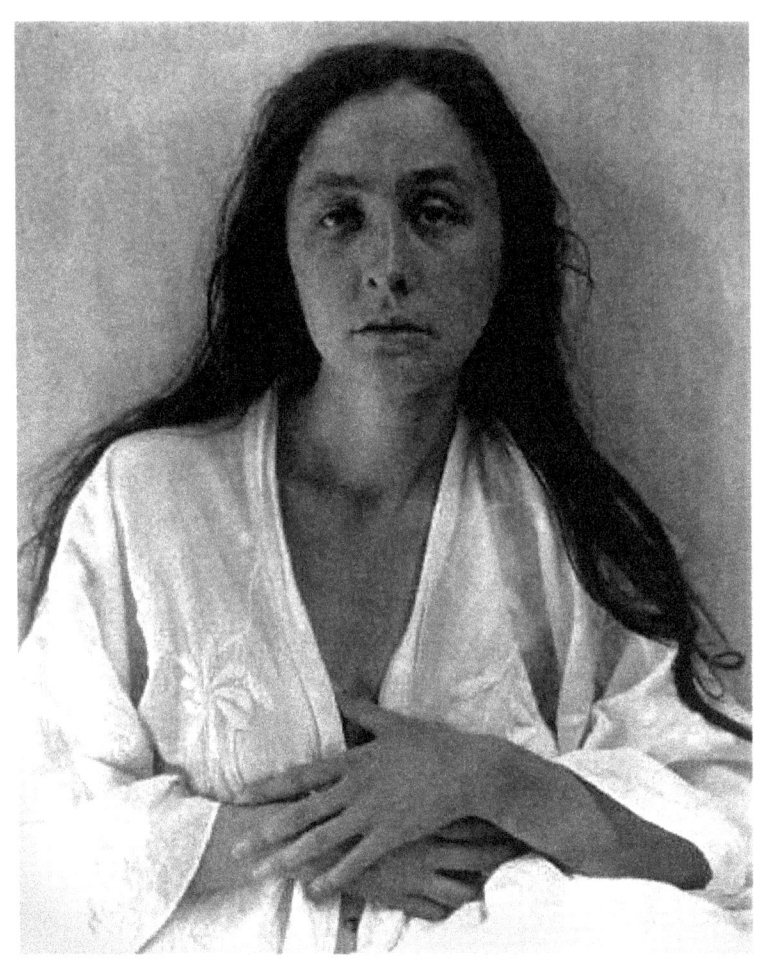

Alfred Stiegliz, *Georgia O'Keeffe*

Assonances

You appeared
from ledges
sheltered
by rough
sensations:

so delicate
and discrete
you offered them
with intense
attention.

Generous
epistolary
assonances
recreated
past
meetings.

With sensual
aesthetics
we bring back
real expectations
of being both
the unique gifts.

Artemisia Lomi Gentileschi, *Danae*

Cosmogony

Celestial vaults
succeeding
to extended births,
cultivating
maternal growths.

Mythical visions, indeed,
unfold
divine beginnings,
to renew
epic narrations,

where gods of heroic deeds
repeat
the universal feast,
celebrating
another pantheist dawn.

The unforeseen,
mutual variations,
however, don't change
the aerated waters inside us,
appearing
in our eternal stories.

John Henry Twachtman, *Enchanted Pool*

Let the Tear Happen

Let the tear happen
after the hypocrite
long wait,
in the opening
occurred
from a withheld
chain.

And be the bare word,
stripped of pride,
to set free
the childish phobia
to blush
at emotional drive,
while expressing
thanks and grateful
plain emotions
to you and to you forever.

Samanta Lai, *Bjork*

Praise to a Free Day

Oh, wind, disperse the oblivion
of wanted tidings,
hesitating with pride
in the grey edge of awakening.

Accept me entirely
from the hanging earth,
that secure enchants
the stasis of fear.

Take me and set me free
from the anchors of the past,
that inflexible bind me
with unsold promises.

Gaetano Previati, *The Dance*

Biographical Notes about the Artists

(In order of appearance)

Hilma af Klint (1862-1944). Swedish painter, a pioneer in the context of abstract art painting. Radical precursor of an art that moves away from the visible reality. She developed since 1906 an abstract language. Her works are not, however, mere utopias of shapes and colours, but rather the representation of what is invisible.

Susana Ragel Nieto (Madrid, 1981). Spanish painter who has won several awards, including: Award Adquisición Virgen de las Viñas de Tomelloso, 2011; First Prize Concurso de Pintura en Directo Fundación de Artes Plásticas Rafael Boti, 2009; Award Gigarpe, Cartagena, 2009. Since 2002, she has presented her works in numerous exhibitions in Spain.
www.ragelnieto.blogspot.com - www.susanaragel.com

Yarek Godfrey (Poland, 1957). Since 1983 he has been living and working between Paris and New York, the city where he has shown his works.
www.yarekgodfrey.com

Caspar David Friedrich (1774-1840). He was a German painter, exponent of romantic art.

Johann Heinrich Füssli (1741-1825). Also known as Henry Fuseli, he was a scholar and Swiss painter of the romantic style, mainly in Britain.

Erwin Blumenfeld (Berlin, 1897 - Rome, 1969). He is considered one of the most representative photographers of the Twentieth century.

Man Ray (1890-1976). Emmanuel Rudzitsky was a painter, photographer and film director, exponent of Dadaism.

Antonio Canova (1757-1822). Italian sculptor and painter, considered the greatest exponent of Neoclassicism and nicknamed as the new Fidia.

František Drtikol (1883-1961). Czech photographer of international importance.

Jean-Frédéric Bazille (1841 - 1870) was a French painter.

Giacomo Balla (1871 - 1958) Italian painter, sculptor and designer, also author of "words in freedom" according to the literary style introduced by Futurism.

Jacob Christian Poen de Wijs (Nijmegen, 1948). He studied at the Royal Academy of Visual Arts in The Hague. He lives and works in the Netherlands.
www.poendewijs.nl - www.detweepauwen.nl

Jean Hippolyte Flandrin (1809-1864). French painter.

François-Auguste-René Rodin (1840-1917). French sculptor and painter.

Simeon Solomon (1840-1905). English painter, adhering to the Pre-Raphaelite movement.

Yves Klein (1928-1962). French artist, forerunner of Body Art, somehow attached to the New Realism.

Pruett Carter (1891-1955). American painter.

Silvana Giordano (Agrigento, 1964). Italian photographer. www.sitohd.com/silvanagiordano

Jean-Joseph Perraud (1819-1876). French sculptor.

Raoul Ubac (1910-1985). French artist: painter, sculptor, photographer and printmaker.

Félix Vallotton (1865-1925). Swiss painter.

Friedrich von Amerling (1803-1887). Austrian painter.

Dante Gabriel Rossetti (1828-1882). British painter and poet, one of the founders of the Pre-Raphaelite movement.

Gwen John (1876-1939). Welsh painter.

Franz von Stuck (1863-1928). German artist: painter and symbolist-expressionist sculptor, illustrator and architect.

Alexander Mijáilovich Rodchenko (1891-1956). Russian painter, photographer and graphic. He contributed to the establishment of the Constructivist movement.

Janos Laszlo Aldor (1895-1944). Hungarian artist.

Cesare Laurenti (1854-1936). Italian painter.

Edward Weston (1886-1958). One of the most important American photographers, operating in the first half of the Twentieth century.

Jeanne Hébuterne (1898-1920). French painter.

Wynn Bullock (1902-1975). He is considered one of the greatest masters of the Twentieth century photography.

Gino Severini (1883-1966). Italian painter who inserted the dynamic values of Futurism into the constructive style of Cubism.

Werner Bischof (1916-1954). Swiss photographer.

Armand Point (1860-1932). French symbolist painter.

Martin Johnson Heade (1819-1904). American painter.

Fjdelisle, pseudonym of François-Julien Delisle. He is a French photographer who posted photos on the Internet (Wikipedia).
www.fjdelisle.net

Alfred Stieglitz (1864-1946). American photographer and gallery owner.

Samanta Lai (Cittadella, Padova, 1977). Italian painter. www.facebook.com/SamLaiPittrice

Maximilián Pirner (1854-1924). Czech painter.

Artemisia Lomi Gentileschi (1593-1653). Italian painter from Caravaggio school.

John Henry Twachtman (1853-1902). American impressionist painter.

Gaetano Previati (1852-1920). Italian painter who, after an early experience in the artistic movement of "Scapigliatura" in Milan, was particularly representative of the artistic movement of "Italian Divisionism".

Photo Credits

- p. 16: © Hilma Af Klint / Wikimedia Commons;

- p. 18: © Susana Ragel Nieto, www.susanaragel.com;

- p. 20: © Yarek Godfrey, www.yarekgodfrey.com;

- p. 22: © Caspar David Friedrich / Wikimedia Commons;

- p. 24: © Johann Heinrich Füssli / Wikimedia Commons;

- p. 26: © Erwin Blumenfeld / Wikimedia Commons;

- p. 28: © Erwin Blumenfeld / Wikimedia Commons;

- p. 30: © Man Ray / Wikimedia Commons;

- p. 32: © Man Ray / Wikimedia Commons;

- p. 34: © Antonio Canova / Wikimedia Commons;

- p. 36: © František Drtikoln / Wikimedia Commons;

- p. 38: © Jean-Frédéric Bazille / Wikimedia Commons;

- p. 40: © Giacomo Balla / Wikimedia Commons;

- p. 42: © Jacob Christian Poen de Wijs, www.poendewijs.nl;

- p. 44: © Jean Hippolyte Flandrin / Wikimedia Commons;

- p. 46: © François-Auguste-René Rodin / Wikimedia Commons;

- p. 48: © Simeon Solomon / Wikimedia Commons;

- p. 50: © Yves Klein / Wikimedia Commons;

- p. 52: © Pruett Carter / Wikimedia Commons;

- p. 56: © Silvana Giordano, www.sitohd.com/silvanagiordano;

- p. 58: © Jean-Joseph Perraud / Wikimedia Commons;

- p. 60: © Raoul Ubac / Wikimedia Commons;

- p. 62: © Félix Vallotton / Wikimedia Commons;

- p. 64: © Friedrich von Amerling / Wikimedia Commons;

- p. 66: © Dante Gabriel Rossetti / Wikimedia Commons;

- p. 68: © František Drtikol, *Painting* / Wikimedia Commons;

- p. 70: © Gwen John / Wikimedia Commons;

- p. 72: © Franz von Stuck / Wikimedia Commons;

- p. 74: © Alexander Mijáilovich Rodchenko / Wikimedia Commons;

- p. 76: © Alexander Mijáilovich Rodchenko / Wikimedia Commons;

- p. 80: © Janos Laszlo Aldor / Wikimedia Commons;

- p. 82: © Cesare Laurenti / Wikimedia Commons;

- p. 84: © Edward Weston / Wikimedia Commons;

- p. 86: © Jeanne Hébuterne / Wikimedia Commons;

- p. 88: © Wynn Bullock / Wikimedia Commons;

- p. 90: © František Drtikoln / Wikimedia Commons;

- p. 92: © Gino Severini / Wikimedia Commons;

- p. 94: © Werner Bischof / Wikimedia Commons;

- p. 96: © Fjdelisle / Wikimedia Commons;

- p. 98: © Armand Point / Wikimedia Commons;

- p. 100: © Martin Johnson Heade / Wikimedia Commons;

- p. 102: © Alfred Stieglitz / Wikimedia Commons;

- p. 104: © Samanta Lai, www.facebook.com/SamLaiPittrice;

- p. 106: © Maxmiliàn Pirner / Wikimedia Commons;

- p. 108: © Alexander Mijáilovich Rodchenko / Wikimedia Commons;

- p. 110: © Alfred Stieglitz / Wikimedia Commons;

- p. 112: © Artemisia Lomi Gentileschi / Wikimedia Commons;

- p. 114: © John Henry Twachtman / Wikimedia Commons;

- p. 116: © Samanta Lai, www.facebook.com/SamLaiPittrice;

- p. 118: © Gaetano Previati / Wikimedia Commons.

OTHER WORKS BY LINO MILITA, PUBLISHED IN ITALIAN

Sogni Sospesi, poems with pictures, some of which in colour: paperback (Youcanprint) and e-book

The tale "Attimo d'Onda" is included in *Le Donne e il Mare* (Youcanprint) paperback and e-book

The poem "Divine Rimostranze" is included in *Gatto, Mon Amour*, (Youcanprint), paperback and e-book

The tale "Crescite Inattese" is included in *Parole di Pane* (Farnesi Editore, paperback)

Translation, from Italian into English, of Cetta De Luca's work *Appunti. Notes from the Heart Poesie e aforismi*

The tale "L'isola che c'è" is included in the e-book *Alla ricerca di Capitan Uncino*

Reciproche Rinascite: my book of poems with pictures (Youcanprint), paperback and e-book, has been translated here with the title *Mutual Rebirths*

Finito di stampare nel mese di Luglio 2015
per conto di Youcanprint *Self-Publishing*

www.ingramcontent.com/pod-product-compliance
Lightning Source LLC
Chambersburg PA
CBHW042336040426
42446CB00021B/3474